I0422899

My First Book About Big Cats

Amazing Animal Books Children's Picture Books

By Molly Davidson

Mendon Cottage Books

JD-Biz Publishing

Download Free Books!
http://MendonCottageBooks.com

All Rights Reserved.
No part of this publication may be reproduced in any form or by any means, including scanning, photocopying, or otherwise without prior written permission from JD-Biz Corp and http://AmazingAnimalBooks.com.
Copyright © 2015

All Images Licensed by Fotolia and 123RF

Read More Amazing Animal Books

Purchase at Amazon.com

Table of Contents

Introduction to Big Cats

Big Cats means any cat that can roar.

Big Cats are carnivores, which means they eat meat.

They do their hunting at night, and lay down to eat.

Lions, cheetahs, and tigers are the three greatest cats of Africa.

Leopards

Leopards will drag their food into a tree to keep it safe.

© kyslynskyy - Fotolia.com

A leopard's tail is almost as long as its body.

Leopards like to be by themselves, they don't like to be with other leopards. Mother leopards will keep their baby cubs with them for 2 years, but then they must live by themselves.

Most leopards are found in South Africa, you may also find some in India, China, and Malaysia.

Wildcats

A wildcat is about the same size as a pet cat.

Most wildcats have a long black stripe down their back.

Endangered Big Cats

The most endangered cats in the World, are the tiger and cheetah.

Some of the reasons that big cats are becoming endangered, dying fast, is poaching (humans killing illegally), where the big cats live is being destroyed, and humans killing for their fur, so they can make clothes.

Where Big Cats Live

© Joanne Stemberger - Fotolia.com

Big cats are adapted to the forest environment. The Bostawa safari is the place where most of these cats live.

Cougars

© hgrose - Fotolia.com

Cougars are also called mountain lions, pumas, and panthers.

Cougars live in the U.S. and Canada, in the Rocky Mountains, and also in parts of South America.

The cougar likes to live where there is lots of thick brush and rocks because it uses these to hide from its prey when it is hunting.

Cougars hunt and live alone.

The cougar is a meat eater, it eats deer, squirrels, raccoons, and sometimes cattle.

Have You Ever Heard Of An Ocelt?

Ocelts love it where it is warm, most of them live in Mexico and South America.

They are about the size of your pet cat.

Some people call them "mini leopards" because of their fur, it looks the same.

© hgrose - Fotolia.com

African Cheetahs

© Anna Omelchenko - Fotolia.com

Cheetahs are the fastest animal in the World.

Cheetahs have claws that can be inside their feet to stuck out, this gives them extra grip when they are running fast.

Cheetahs use their tail to help them make very sharp turns, which help them catch their prey.

The African Caracal

The caracal lives in Africa and Asia.

The word caracal means black-eared in Turkish, they have long ears with black fur sticking out the top.

© Duncan Noakes - Fotolia.com

They eat meat, such as rodents, birds, and even small antelope.

The average life of the caracal is 19 years, in the wild.

Caracals like to live by themselves, except the babies stay with the mother for the first year of their life.

What Big Cats Eat

© Eric Gevaert - Fotolia.com

They mainly eat meat, this gives them proteins and fat.

Cubs Or Baby Big Cats

Cubs are in their mothers for 4 months before they are born.

© Alan Lucas - Fotolia.com

Cubs of a lion are born in a litter (group) of one baby up to six babies!

Cubs drink their mother's milk for 6 months, but they start eating meat, as well as milk, at 3 months.

Cubs begin hunting at about one year old.

Tigers

The tiger the biggest cat in the World.

 It is the third largest meat eater in the World, behind the brown bear, and polar bear.

Tigers live for 20 - 26 years, in the wild or in a zoo.

A Cat Called a Serval

Servals are very skinny cats, but they are not the smallest of the big cats.

© Sarah Cheriton-Jones - Fotolia.com

Servals like it to be very hot, that is why they all live in Africa.

Snow Leopards: King of The Frozen Mountains

© veneratio - Fotolia.com

The snow leopard is a rare cat from the mountains of Asia.

Their thick fur is perfect for keeping warm in their cold mountain home.

They also have a long tail to help them balance as they hop from rock to rock.

They eat mountain sheep, rabbits, birds, and if they get hungry enough, they will eat grass and twigs.

Snow leopards live by themselves, except mother leopards who will raise their babies on their own inside a den.

The Bobcat

Bobcats live near the Canadian border and throughout the U.S. and Mexico.

Bobcats are awake at night, so humans normally don't see them.

© JackF - Fotolia.com

They live for about 13 years.

Bobcats like to be alone, and cubs leave their mother when they are just 10-12 months old.

Rabbits, squirrels, and rodents are what they eat.

The Jaguarundi

The Jaguarundi is also known as the "otter cat."

They have very powerful legs. They use them to jump far distances.

Unlike most big cats, Jaguarundis are all one color, no spots or stripes.

The Lynx - A Majestic Cat

© byrdyak - Fotolia.com

Lynx have big paws, with soft fur on the bottom, and in between their toes. The fur helps keep them warm when walking on the snow.

Lynx means "brightness," this is where their name came from, because their eyes look like they glow in the dark!

Pumas

Pumas have bright green eyes, and there front legs are shorter than their back legs.

Pumas can be found in Africa, Asia, and also in America.

They live in areas that have forests, swamps, and are grassy.

They eat deer, but will also eat birds and rabbits and other smaller animals.

A puma can jump up to 20 feet which makes them hard to catch.

Jaguars

Jaguars live in South America, around the Amazon River.

© S.R.Miller - Fotolia.com

They have big padded paws that let them move quietly through the forest, and sometimes they will climb into trees to sleep or hunt.

Jaguars like to hunt at night. They have very good eyesight and sharp teeth.

They like eat over 80 different kinds of small animals, and sometimes fish or turtles.

Lions

Lions are the second largest cat, behind the tiger.

The boy lions weigh about 400 pounds.

© Lsantilli - Fotolia.com

When lions are angry or want attention they roar loudly.

Most lions live in Africa and live in groups which are called prides.

Lions live for about 12 years in the wild, if they are not hurt or attacked.

Conclusion

We hope you have learned many things about big cats.

Download Free Books!
http://MendonCottageBooks.com

Publisher

JD-Biz Corp

P O Box 374

Mendon, Utah 84325

http://www.jd-biz.com/

www.ingramcontent.com/pod-product-compliance
Lightning Source LLC
Chambersburg PA
CBHW050841290526
45792CB00001B/487